Choose Your Own Path to Publication

Flowable Books (e-books, Audio)

Fixed-Format Books (Print, Read-to-me)

Stephanie Neilan

Copyright 2020 by Hearth Publications
All rights reserved
Email HearthPublications@gmail.com
for rights and permissions or to contact the author.

Aaaand done! Whew! I just finished final edits on my literary project. I gave it to my friends, family, and favorite grammar geeks in a bid to make it the best it could be. My nonfiction is informative, my fiction is exciting, and my poetry is touching.

In short, I have created a masterpiece that deserves to be read multiple times. I could keep this all to myself, but I am feeling brave. It's time to allow the world a chance to get their own copy.

There are so many paths to choose from, however. What is the best way to share my book? What skills, programs, and resources will I need? How do I start? What is the best way to go from finishing my story to producing it as a book?

There are different things that will have to be done depending on the path I chose to take. As I make those decisions, I know I will end up with a product that I can be proud of.

I start by looking at the text. My words are perfect, but what about my formatting? Did I use style guides to differentiate my "normal" text from my "heading" chapters?

If not, then I can take care of that in most word programs. In Microsoft, I can find the list of styles on the home tab.

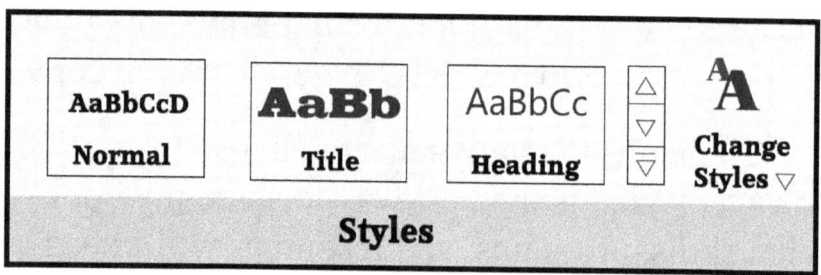

Even Google docs has it! When I click on the arrow by the current style, other options appear.

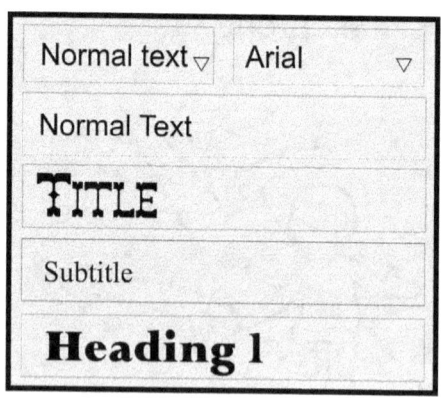

I like to link my text to a style because then I can automatically adjust things like text size, font, and indents by simply updating the style guide.

I also like to "insert" page breaks between chapters and picture book pages. (I sometimes insert the break after I've hit the enter button 4 times so it FOR SURE ends up on a new page.)

Now it's time for my first big decision. Do I want to make a "fixed-format" book, "flowable" book, or have it be strictly audio?

If I create something in fixed form, then I don't need to worry about things shifting around when people read my story on different sized devices. This is particularly nice if the way the text looks or is placed on the page is important (like with shape poems and picture books). Not only can I ultimately transform it into a .pdf or .kpf (kindle create) e-file, I can also use it for print copies.

A flowable book won't make the e-file to print transition as easily, but it is how most e-books are formatted because it allows the readers to read at their preferred text size. No magnifying glasses needed!

Audio books, by contrast, are heard — not seen. The type of file I produce only matters if the narrator cares.

Decision Time

For "Fixed-Format," go to page 5.

For "Flowable," go to page 9.

For "Audio," go to page 13.

Fixed-Format Books

I've decided that a fixed-format layout will be the best fit for my current book project.

Because I can't change the way a page looks simply by tilting a screen, I have to decide what shape I want my book to be: rectangle or square.

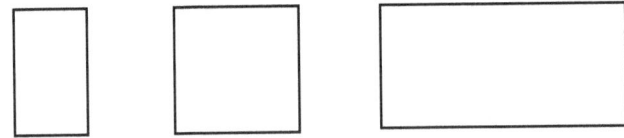

Once I've chosen the basic shape, I might as well commit to a size. I can adjust the page in "page setup." Google docs doesn't have the same flexibility other word processors do, but I can adjust the margins and pretend those lines are my pages until I can transfer my project into a program that WILL make the page size I want.

Page setup		X
Orientation	Margins (inches)	
Portrait Landscape	Top	1
Paper Size		
Letter (8.5" x 11")	Bottom	1
Tabloid (11" x 17")		
Legal (8.5" x 14")	Left	1
Statement (5.5" x 8.5")		
Executive (7.25" x 10.5")		

But how do I know that the size I have chosen is a good one? I can compare it to what's already out there. Barnes and Noble has a list on their website of traditional book sizes.*

Fiction and Narrative non-fiction:

4" x 6", 4.25" x 7", 4.37" x 7", 5" x 8", 5.06" x 7.81", 5.25" x 8", 5.5" x 8.25", 5.5" x 8.5", 5.83" x 8.27", 6" x 9", and 6.14" x 9.21".

Cookbooks and other designed books:

7" x 10", 7.5" x 9.25", 8" x 8", 8" x 10", 8.25" x 11", 8.268" x 11.693", 8.5" x 8.5", and 8.5" x 11".

Children's books:

11" x 8.5", 8.25" x 11", and 8.268" x 11.693".

But not every printing company makes every sized book. Companies that print large runs of books (hundreds at a time), usually allow more sizes than Print On Demand Companies (PODs). But nobody I know makes 8 foot tall books. Signs? Yes. But not books.

Maybe one day.

*https://help.barnesandnoble.com/app/answers/detail/a_id/4047/kw/nook%20press%20paper%20copies%20books

When making my final decision, I also want to think about who is going to be sending out my books to buyers. I could set up a website with an attached PayPal account and ship the books on my own, but if I want someone else to do that work for me, then I need to know if they have distribution restrictions.

If I publish through Amazon, for example, they will make it available for sale through their website. But they will only share my print book's information with other sites like Barnes and Noble if it's one of their "expanded distribution" sizes.*

The sizes they support in the expanded program are:

Books with color interiors:

5.5" x 8.5", 6" x 9", 6.14" x 9.21", 7" x 10", 8" x 10", 8.5" x 8.5", and 8.5" x 11".

Books without color interiors on white paper:

5" x 8", 5.06" x 7.81", 5.25" x 8", 5.5" x 8.5", 6" x 9", 6.14" x 9.21", 6.69" x 9.61", 7" x 10", 7.44" x 9.69", 7.5" x 9.25", 8" x 10", 8.5" x 11".

*https://kdp.amazon.com/en_US/help/topic/GQT T4W3T5AYK7L45

Luckily, there are some overlaps.

Fiction:

5" x 8" (black and white) 5.06" x 7.81" (black and white) , 5.25" x 8" (black and white) , 5.5" x 8.5" (black and white / color), 6" x 9" (black and white / color), 6.14" x 9.21" (black and white / color).

Cookbooks and other designed books:

7" x 10" (black and white / color), 7.5" x 9.25" (black and white), 8" x 10" (black and white / color), 8.5" x 8.5" (color), and 8.5" x 11" (black and white / color).

When I know the exact size of my book, I can start thinking about the layout. Many books look fine with nothing inside but words, but biographies, kid books, and even some poetry and text books benefit from images that complement the text.

As I decide what goes where, I think about how many images I want to add, where I want them to go, and what size I need.

Go to "Pictures" on page 17.

Flowable Books

Flowable books are e-books. The books will be seen on many different screen sizes with changing font sizes. Because of this, I have to think about what looks good on a small screen as well as a large screen.

One of the first things I do is update my "normal" text's style guide. To do this, I can right click when my mouse is over the name of the style I want to format. A list of options will appear. I will then chose to "modify" the text. At the bottom of the page it will ask what part of the style I want to "format."

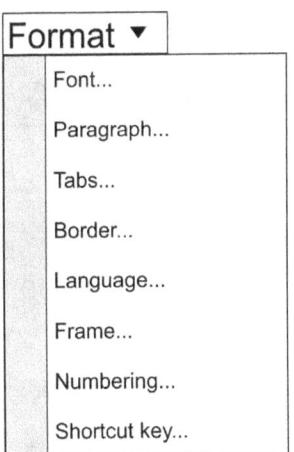

I focus on adjusting the "paragraph" first. I have the option to make the "first lines" special by automatically indenting them. (No tabs required.) I then set the measurement to between .25" and .33" depending on my mood. If it's bigger than that, then I think it looks odd when I'm reading it on my phone. I can make other adjustments (New font? Different size? Centered? Bolded?) in the same general area.

Another thing I can do is to take a section of text that has already been marked with the appropriate style name, make it perfect, select it, right click, and then "update [current style] to Match Selection."

```
A    Update Heading 1 to Match Selection
     Modify...
     Select All 1 Instance(s)
     Rename...
     Remove from Quick Style Gallery
     Add Gallery to Quick Access Toolbar
```

Having the "headings" or chapter titles clearly marked will also help when making a table of contents. I can insert one myself or use a program that will look at my style guide to automatically create one for me.

If I am using a program like PagePlus, all I have to do to create my table of contents is to "insert" one. It will then scan my document and create a list with all the words I tagged as "headings." Draft2Digital will also automatically scan for that designation and create a table of contents with links for me.

But sometimes I feel like doing it myself. When that mood strikes, I create hyperlinks. I highlight the text in the table of contents, and right click. I then choose the "hyperlink" option which will allow me to link to a "place in this document" where all my chapter headings show up. Once I click on the appropriate heading, the computer will make the connection.

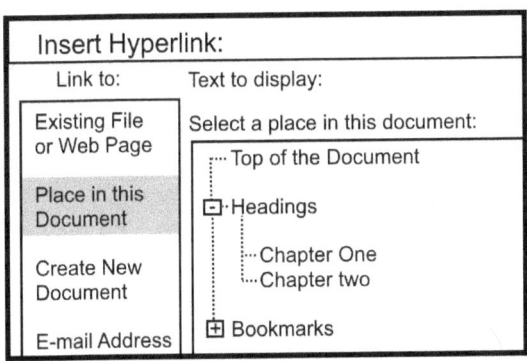

Ta da!

To finish my book, I will still need a cover. Tables, family photos, and other pictures that support what's happening in the story can also make the contents easier to understand and/or more personable.

Go to "Pictures" on page 17.

Audio Books

Many people like to listen to stories while they clean, drive, sew, etc. In order for them to enjoy the story, it must be told with expression. If I'm not in the mood to channel my inner drama queen, or if I was only a drama peon at best, I might need to hire someone else to create the audio files for me.

Before I hire them, I can listen to a sample of their work to make sure they have the right voice for the project. They can be found through ACX, Findaway Voices, Fiverr...

Some of ACX's requirements (a place that publishes audio books) include:

All mono or all stereo files

192 kbps or higher MP3

Constant bit rate (CBR) at 44.1 kHz

Between -23dB and -18dB RMS

No distracting background noises

"Quiet time" at the beginning and end of each audio section.

Whether I hire it out or do it myself, I will want to make my pages easy to read. This means adjusting the font/print size until the words are clear and distinct. I can then read from the computer, or print it off. Some narrators like the flow of .doc files, while others prefer .pdf files so they don't accidentally mess something up.

To save something as a .pdf, all I have to do is click "save as" and request the .pdf option.

Google docs hides their .pdf under the "download" tab.

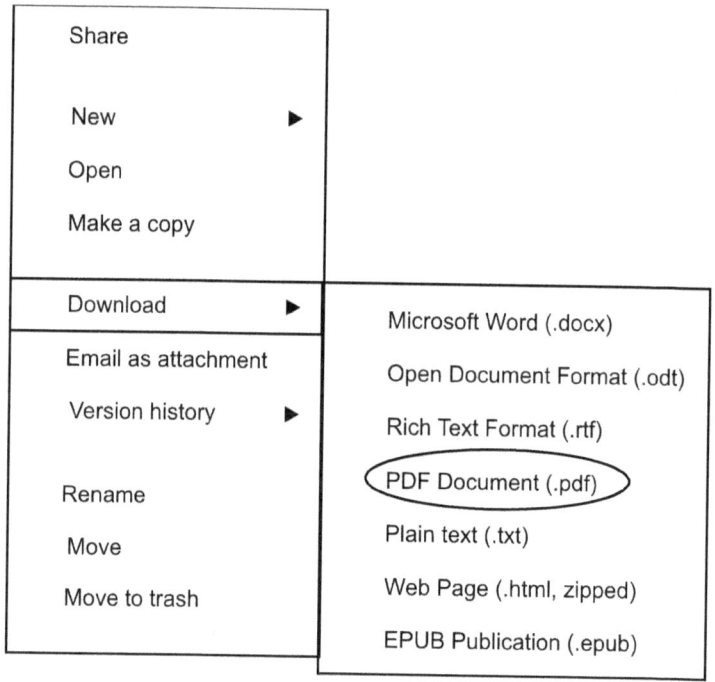

If I decide to record it myself, I can add notes or highlight when different people are speaking, if I think it will help my performance.

When recording, I like my work area to be as sound proof as possible. Some libraries have recording rooms, but small, carpeted closets with lots of clothes can also be used.

When narrating, I try to make each chapter its own "track," and I think it's easiest to do that if I record the entire chapter in one session. I can then edit and "clean" the files in programs like Obi and Audacity.

While I could record my audio using a computer's built-in-microphone, the quality usually isn't as good as what an external microphone can produce.

Once I have my audio files, I upload them to my audio book producer like Findaway Voices or ACX where they are often double checked for quality.

As much as I wish I was now done, I'm not. I still need a cover to go with my CD. If I go with ACX, for example, the cover size they want is 8" x 8" (300 dpi).

Go to "Pictures" on page 17.

Pictures

Even if I have no interior pictures, I will always need a cover. Book cover sizes will vary, but most e-books accept 5" x 8", 300 dpi (Dots Per Inch) images.

Some interior images/drawings/photos, especially with fixed-format books, will also have to be specific sizes. Sometimes I will add pictures to a story or take them away because of how they affect the layout.

Once I decide where the pictures are going and the size I need, it's time to gather them. I just have to decide where I am going to start looking first.

Decision Time

To create the pictures myself, go to page 19.

To outsource my artwork, go to page 25.

To use what is already out there, go to page 27.

Pictures Made By Myself

As an artist, I can shade with the best of them, and there isn't any medium that scares me. Even though I know that I will ultimately need a digital file, sometimes I prefer to create something on paper or canvas first. Call me old fashioned. It's okay.

Decision Time

To create the pictures with a pencil, paint brush, tissue paper, etc. go to page 21.

To create the picture with a digital program, go to page 23.

Non-digital Artwork

I won't go into the details of how I made my artwork so amazing, but it is glorious to behold and perfect for my book.

Now I just have to get it into digital form. Two options that come to mind involve using a camera or a scanner. Both will save it as a picture.

With a camera, I have to be very careful with lighting and angles because I want the best, clearest representation of my work.

I can't adjust the angle of a scanner, but if my art is flat, I wouldn't want to. I just need a good scanner that can preserve the quality of my work. Alas, even the best scanners have size limitations so that is something else I have to keep in mind.

Go to "Adjustments" on page 29.

Digital Artwork

Since I can create what I want either way, why make more work for myself? I begin by opening up my favorite drawing app. There are several to chose from: MediBang, Phototshop, Gimp, Paint.net, etc.

Once I open my program, I check the image size. I want to make sure the picture will be 300 dpi and fit its assigned slot when I'm done.

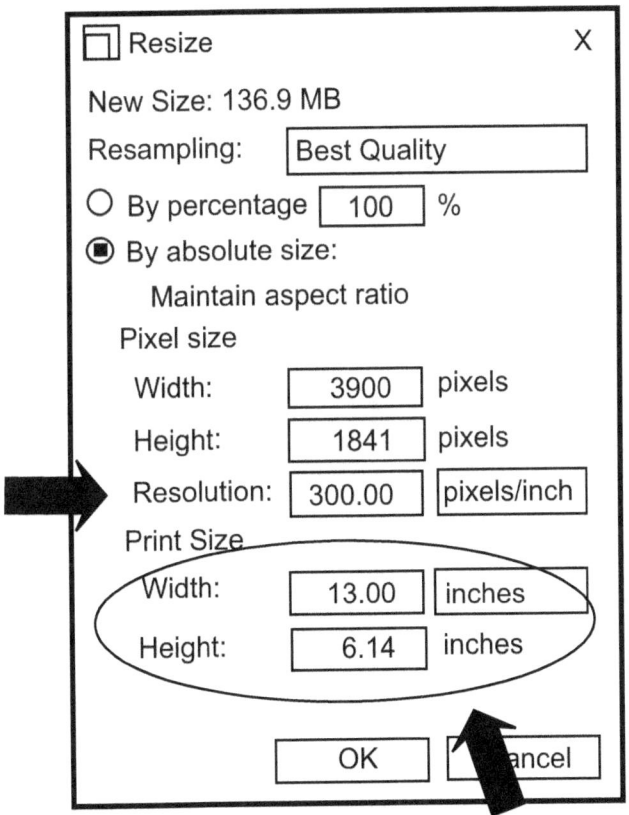

Do I need a 13" x 6" picture?

Then, I create my image.

If there is a transparent section I want to keep that way, I save it as a .png. If I want to easily resize it in the future, I save it as an .eps or .svg (vector). If it's a normal picture, I save it as a .jpg file. Unfortunately, not every drawing program will open/save vector pictures, so if that's what I want, I need to make sure my program can do it.

Go to "Adjustments" on page 29.

Outsourced Artwork

I can draw stick figures, but that's about it. Since I don't HAVE to do everything, I'm going to go to sites like fiverr and find an artist who can make the custom pictures this book needs to shine.

When I hire them, I will:

*Confirm how long it will take before I get the finished artwork.

*Ask for high resolution results.

*Request the copyright (or "free use" to print as many copies as I will need for the chosen book and associated promotional materials).

Go to "Adjustments" on page 29.

Artwork Already Out There

I know I need art, but it doesn't need to be custom work so I start my search on-line. I have to be very careful, however, because even though some pictures are free to use, others are copyrighted or have resolutions too low to be helpful.

Some sites (like Depositphotos and Shutterstock) specialize in getting high-resolution pictures into the hands of those who need them. They aren't free, but they come with the model releases, and the right to modify and use the photos commercially.

Other places, like pixabay, clipart-library.com, and photosforclass.com have pictures from people willing to take pity on the poor art-starved soul. They don't have the same selection, but if I find what I need — Wahoo!

If I don't want to go directly to a specific website, I can do a search online. I like to use Bing because the "license" filter associated with its image search allows me to look for pictures based on their copyright (public domain, free to share and use, free to modify, etc.)

I target pictures that I can modify and use commercially. While the system works well, a few copyrighted pictures might slip through the filter, so I have to double check the origin site.

Even if the picture is legally okay to use, that doesn't mean it is the size that I need. To find its dimensions, I open it with a photo editing program and look for details about the image. If I expand a picture too far beyond its original settings, it will look blurry.

Not so cute now, is he?

Go to "Adjustments" on page 29.

Adjustments

Now that I have my pictures, I usually have to make some minor adjustments.

The most common adjustments I make involve trimming, adding text, and merging images.

To trim, I right click on the image, go to format, and then look for the "crop" symbol.

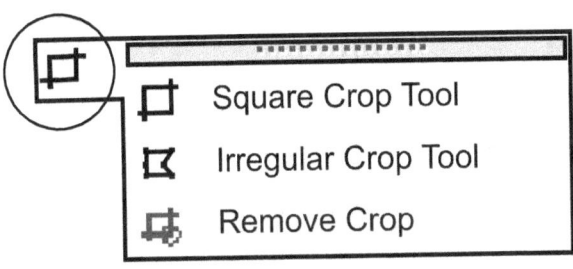

Some programs only allow for straight line cuts, but this example also has an "irregular crop" option. I just trim the picture until it's honed in on the section I want and delete the rest.

Some programs also have an "eraser" option that allows me to remove things pixel by pixel.

I personally use a photo editor program when I want to add text. I open up the picture within the software program and double check that it is the size and resolution I want.

I then add a "layer" so my changes will be easy to delete/modify. Layers start as a transparent plane. A checkerboard pattern will appear in the transparent areas if the plane is isolated.

Once I add my image, or in this case text, it will appear on top of the "background." I can move it around the base picture until I find the size/font/position that I think works best. I then save the picture.

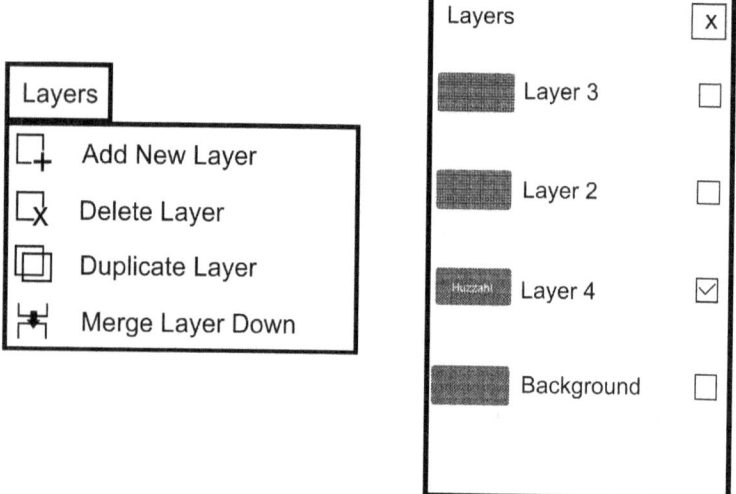

If I am adding more than one element, I will sometimes put each component of the picture on its own layer. All of the top layer is seen, and the rest of the picture emerges as the program works its way down the layers. I can make specific layers temporarily invisible by clicking on the box next to their name.

Layers also allow me to do some cool tricks when merging images.

For example, the swan in this picture was isolated on its own layer before I made its entire plane partially transparent. The final image was then "merged" together into a single .jpg file. I can also use layers to add shadows at the base of inserted images so the union feels more natural.

Some programs also have blending tools so the slight variations in color from one image to the next bleed into one another more naturally.

I can also use other features like the "Gaussian blur" to soften edges or add highlights. Experimenting can be fun!

When making the cover, I MUST NOT forget to include the title of the book and the author's name.

Decision Time

To add interior pictures to a flowable file, go to page 33.

To add interior pictures to a fixed format file, go to page 35.

To publish a flowable book, go to page 37.

To publish an audio book, go to page 39.

To publish a fixed-format book, go to page 41.

Adding Interior Pictures in a Flowable File

To attach the pictures in flowable files, I "insert" them from wherever I had saved their digital file.

I then make sure that they are positioned between the words I want them positioned between by right clicking on the picture and choosing "format." There are several "text wrapping" options, but I like positioning the text so it only appears above and below the picture, or "top and bottom."

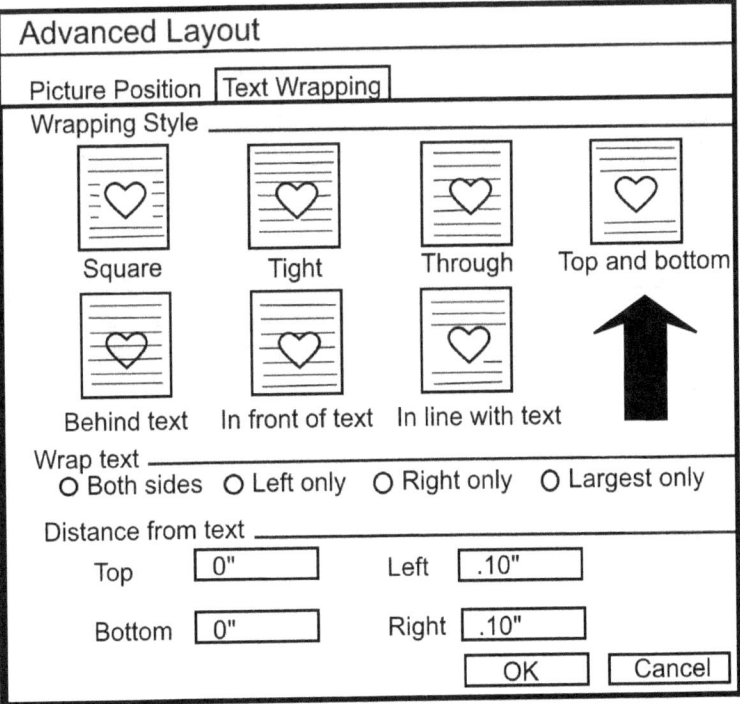

I then "anchor" it to the preceding text. I can also center it to the page, but that command doesn't always get translated. At least the picture is attached to the words and will move if they do (such as when the reader adjusts the size).

```
Advanced Layout
┌─────────────────┬──────────────┐
│ Picture Position │ Text Wrapping │
└─────────────────┴──────────────┘
Horizontal
  ○ Alignment          [Left]      relative to   [Column]
  ○ Book layout        [Inside]    of            [Margin]
  ○ Absolute Position  [0"]        to the right of [Column]
  ○ Relative Position  [    ]      relative to   [Page]
Vertical
  ○ Alignment          [Top]       relative to   [Page]
  ○ Absolute Position  [0"]        below         [Paragraph]
  ○ Relative Position  [    ]      relative to   [Page]
Options
  ☐ Move object with text    ☐ Allow overlap
  ☐ Lock anchor              ☐ Layout in table cell

                              [ OK ]  [ Cancel ]
```

Go to "Publishing a Flowable Book" on page 37.

Adding Interior Pictures in a Fixed-Format file

For fixed-format books, I like to use Page Plus because it's "facing pages" feature helps me visualize it in book form better, but I can do what I need to in other word processors.

With the book page size already chosen, I just have to insert the pictures and manipulate them with the text until everything looks perfect.

I can choose between having margins around everything ("no bleed") or having pictures go to the very edge of the page ("bleed").

Ultimately, I'll want to publish/save it as a .pdf, but sometimes the program will want to "compress" my pictures. That's why I like to double check those settings before I publish/save.

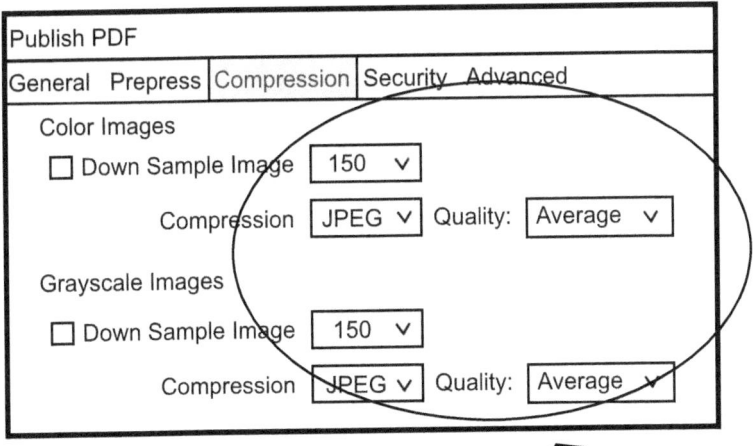

I can do better than that!

Go to "Publishing a Fixed-Format Book" on page 41.

Publishing a Flowable Book

Ah, the text is perfect, the cover is perfect, and any pictures that I inserted are anchored perfectly. It's time to turn my files into an ebook!

Jutoh (http://jutoh.com) and Calibre (https://calibre-ebook.com) are an example of two programs that will compile the books without forcing me to use a specific distributor. However, not every distributor likes Calibre's software so it works on a personal level, but not the professional one. Sigh.

Some places that will compile it into an e-book for me that also have a built in distribution system include Amazon (https://kdp.amazon.com), Barnes and Noble (https://press.barnesandnoble.com), Draft2digital (https://draft2digital.com), and Smashwords (https://www.smashwords.com).

To publish, I go to their site and begin a new book. I upload my "interior" files (.doc or .docx depending on the system) and cover (.jpg file) before filling out some details related to the book. They want to know things like the title, author name, and genre. They will also ask for a blurb (those enticing paragraphs one sees on the back of a book to get people to read more).

Another thing the distributors will ask about is an ISBN number. This is the book's unique identifier. No matter where the book is sold, the ISBN number will stay the same. This helps with recording purposes.

The places that offer to compile AND distribute it for me will often allow me to use one of their ISBN numbers for free. This lists them as the publisher or imprint used to create the book. If I don't want them listed, I can purchase my own ISBN number through Bowker.

If I want to publish my book in more than one format (for example, e-book AND print), then I will need to purchase a separate ISBN for each edition.

To learn more about ISBNs, go to https://www.isbn.org.

Go to "Finale" on page 55.

Publishing an Audio Book

Now that I have my audio files prepped and my cover ready, I need to find the best way to share it with the world. I could make "hard" copies by recording it directly onto a CD.

I can also upload it on-line for those who want to get digital a download of it. Both Findaway Voices and ACX have distribution options to make it easy on me. For them, I simply create a new project, attach a blurb, and upload my audio files and book cover.

The blurb is essentially an advertisement for the project. What will the listener gain from my book? Knowledge? An escape? Words to woo their love?

Go to "Finale" on page 55.

Publishing a Fixed-Format Book

Now that I have my fixed-format files, I have to decide if I want to make it an e-book, print book, or read-to-me book.

Decision Time

To publish as a print book, go to page 43.

To publish as an e-book, go to page 47.

Publishing a Print Book

Sometimes I want a book I can read in the tub without fear of electrocuting myself which is why this book is destined to be printed with ink.

When I am making a print book, I like to start by adjusting my margins. The original file had even margins all around the text, but it won't look even in a print book because the shadows in the middle of the book will make it look off centered. The thicker the book, the more "inside margin" space I want. For most books, I am happy with .6" for the middle of the book and .4" on the outside edges.

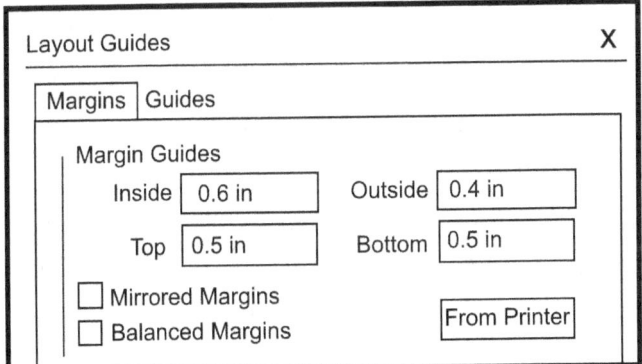

Some PODs (Print On Demand companies), like Amazon, will only do soft cover books while others, like Ingramspark and Barnes and Noble, will offer hard copy options.

Other will also have a minimum page count. Barnes and Noble's POD lets me go as low as 18 pages, but Amazon requires at least 24.

Knowing my page count, page size, and what kind of cover I want helps me determine what publisher I should use.

Once I know the publisher I want, I look at their cover requirements. The cover is, essentially, one giant picture with the front cover, spine, and back cover all together. The front cover is on the right side, the spine is in the middle, and the back is on the left side.

To make the cover, I need to know the exact page count. Black and white colored pages are smaller than pages used for color ink, so I need to pay attention to the difference so I can get an accurate spine width. I also need to add about an extra .125 inches to each edge of the picture for trimming error (.25 total trim error).

Height = Height + .25,

Width = Width x 2 + .25 + Spine

Spine = # of pages x ½ page thickness

For example, if I am creating a black and white 5" x 8" book with 106 pages through amazon, then...

Height = 8" + .25" = 8.25"

Width = 5" x 2 + .25" (trim error) + 106 (pages) x 0.002252" (width of ½ a page) = 10.49"

Once I know the dimensions, I open my photo editor/publishing program and set the size I need. I then add vertical and horizontal guidelines to help ensure the book looks the way it's supposed to.

The guidelines lines for my hypothetical book are:

Horizontal: .125" and 8.125"

Vertical: .125", 5.125", 5.37", and 10.37"

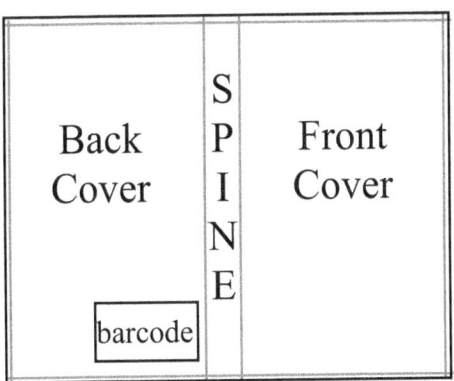

A blurb for the whole book goes on the back portion of the cover. As I write it, I think about what the readers will want to know. What kind of book is it? What will they discover while they read?

When creating the cover I also need to leave room for a barcode in the bottom right corner of the back cover. If I don't provide my own ISBNed barcode, the printer will create one for me.

I can go to page 17 to remind me how to create a cover picture. Afterward, I will save the final product as a .pdf. ("save as" .pdf)

Then I got to my publisher and upload my interior files, my cover, and answer some questions about the book.

They will also ask if I have an ISBN number. It's what the booksellers will use to distinguish my book from the others. If I don't, some places will offer to give me one for free. If I do decide to purchase my own, then I will need to get more than one if I plan to publish my book more than one way. (Details related to ISBNs can be found at https://www.isbn.org.)

Go to "Finale" on page 55.

Publishing a Fixed-Format E-Book

All my pages look perfect so I can save it as a .pdf file. A lot of e-readers accept .pdf files so I can think of it as a finished product. They treat each page like a picture so the reader might have to zoom in if the print is small and they are trying to read it on a small device, but they don't need a specific nook or kindle app to access it, which is really nice.

I can either set up a shop on my own website and distribute it myself/through a program, or I can upload it to distribution sites that accept .pdf files. Sadly, not all of them will, but Amazon's kindle direct press will.

As convenient as that is, sometimes, it's nice to hear someone else read the story as I "turn" the pages. I can create read-to-me books using Amazon's Kindle Book Creator.

Decision Time

To call it good, go to "Finale" on page 55.

To create a Read -to-me Book, go to page 49.

Publishing a Read-to-Me Book

I really wanted to have the option to hear and see the book at the same time, so I begin the process the same way I would begin an audio book.

First, I determine who the narrator will be. If I decide to outsource it, great, otherwise, I will have to remind myself to read with expression!*

I will also want high quality sound files when I am done. Some requirements ACX (an audio book publisher) has for their tracks include:

All mono or all stereo files

192 kbps or higher MP3

Constant bit rate (CBR) at 44.1 kHz

Between -23dB and -18dB RMS

No distracting background noises

"Quiet time" at the beginning and end of each audio section.

*Narrators can be found through ACX, Findaway Voices, Fiverr...

Whether I hire it out or do it myself, I will want to make my pages easy to read. Some narrators prefer to receive a .pdf copy of the file so they don't erase something by accident.

To save something as a .pdf, all I have to do is click "save as" and request the .pdf option. Google docs hides their .pdf under the "download" tab.

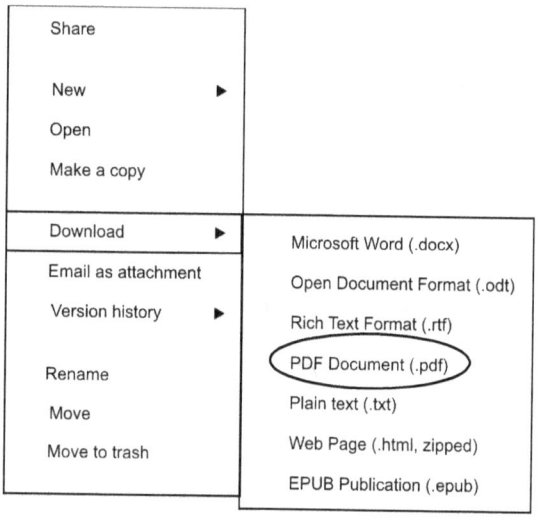

If I want to add notes or highlight when different people are speaking, I can do that as well if I think it will help my performance.

When recording, I like my work area to be as sound proof as possible. Some libraries have recording rooms, but small, carpeted closets with lots of clothes are not bad options.

When narrating, I record one page at a time. Each page becomes its own "track" that I can edit and "clean" in programs like Obi and Audacity.

While I could record my audio using a computer's built-in-microphone, the quality usually isn't as good as what an external microphone can produce.

Once I have my audio files, I prepare to make my book using Amazon's free Kindle Create software program. I think it is the easiest, non-app way to produce a read-to-me story. It allows me to attach my audio files to the individual .pdf pages so when the reader presses the page's sound icon, the narration for that text will play.

There are three book creator options available from the start up page, so I have to be careful to pick the "textbook" option.

```
Ⓚ Kindle Create
File  Edit  View  Help

    Select the type of book you are making      Upload a print ready PDF which
        ☐  Novels, Essays, poetry                can be enhanced to reference
                                                 other material.
        ☐  Comics with Guided View               Use Kindle Create to add:
                                                     Video and Audio
        ☐  Textbooks, Cookbooks,                     Image Pop-ups
           Travel Guides                             Weblinks

                                                [ Choose File ]    [ Cancel ]
```

When my book project file opens, I upload the .pdf story file. Once it shows up, I click on the page I want and begin uploading its corresponding audio.

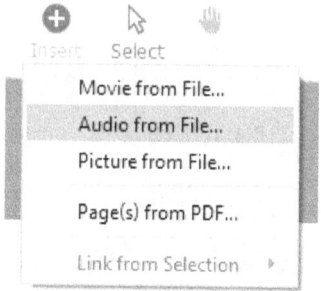

I then decide if I want the audio functions to be visible or not. If I do, then I request the "Full Player" and use an icon button for the appearance. If I don't, then I use the "Play/Pause" player style and change the appearance of the button to "invisible."

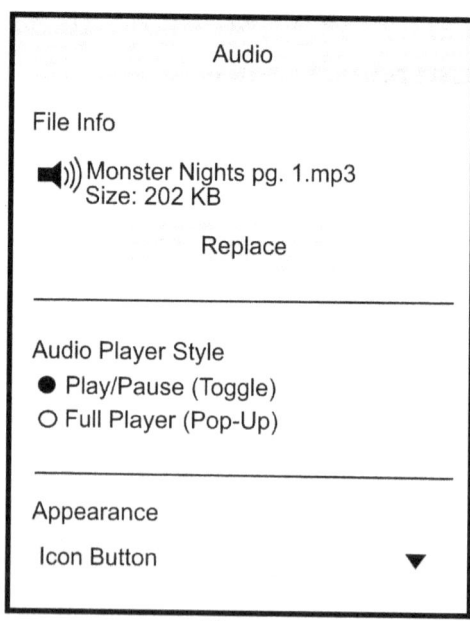

I then place the buttons where the reader would think to press them.

When I'm done, I can preview it before compiling it to make sure I attached the right files to the correct page. I then take it to kdp.amazon.com, answer their questions about my book, upload the "interior" files (.kpf) and cover, write a blurb (the book appetizer that entices the reader to want to know more), and either use their ISBN or upload one of my own. (Learn more about ISBNs at www.isbn.org.)

Because this file is more intricate than a regular e-book, not every e-book reader can handle it. For example, my basic kindle reader won't open it, my phone app will open it but won't play the sound, and my kindle fire will open it with the ability to play the sounds. They might fix that in the future, but that's what happened last time I made one.

Go to "Finale" on page 55.

Finale

Now that I have created my wonderful book and uploaded it, I preview it one last time before approving it. Now all that's left is setting a price. The pricing screen should let me know the minimum price I can set it at and what my expected royalties would be.

If this is my first book through the site, I will also have to add banking and tax information so that I get paid. ;D

It's my work, my baby, and the government recognizes that. But any future legal battles will be easier if I have an official copyright from the government. I can apply for one at https://www.copyright.gov.

I promise to take care of that in the morning, but for now I am going to celebrate. I published my book!!!

Reference Page

DPI - **D**ots **P**er **I**nch

POD - **P**rint **O**n **D**emand

ISBN - **I**nternational **S**tandard **B**ook **N**umber, Learn more at www.isbn.org.

Copyright - Government recognized creation claim. Learn more at www.copyright.gov.

Some Word Processors

    Microsoft

    Google Docs

    LibreOffice

    PagePlus

Some Publishing Places
- Books
    - Kdp (https://kdp.amazon.com/)
    - Nook Press (press.barnesandnoble.com/)
    - IngramSpark (www.ingramspark.com)
- E-book Only
    - Draft2Digital(draft2digital.com/)
    - Smashwords (www.smashwords.com/)
    - Calibre (https://calibre-ebook.com)
    - Jutoh (jutoh.com)
- Audio
    - Findaway Voices
    - ACX

Some E-book File Types
- .epub (nook)
- .mobi (kindle)
- .pdf (e-reader)
- .kpf (kindle create)

Some Picture File Types

    .png (for transparent sections)

    .eps/.svg (for pictures that resize easily)

    .jpg (regular pictures)

Some Digital Drawing Programs

    MediBang

    Photoshop

    Paint.net

    Gimp

Some Places to Find Photos

    Depositphotos

    Shutterstock

    Pixabay

    clipart-library.com

    photosforclass.com

Blurb

The book summary typically found on the back cover. Sometimes accented with endorsements, it gets the reader excited for what they will get with their purchase.

For fiction books, blurbs include a description of the main character, what they want, what stands in their way, and their time limit (if any).

For nonfiction books, this will summarize what the reader will get to learn.

For poetry, the blurb should let the readers know the type, tone, and theme of the poems.

www.ingramcontent.com/pod-product-compliance
Lightning Source LLC
Chambersburg PA
CBHW070318220526
45465CB00004B/1903